AF471653

You are free to share and distribute this book.

it was written and compiled in the winter of 2013 and 2014 in a small house which reeked of diesel fumes in Preston, Idaho.

Yellow Mountain Collective 2014

yellowmountaincollective.com

Dedicated to my Idaho guru Charles Potts

Evil

There's no such thing as a bad person,
just bad people with bad ideas.

Evil is what happens when ignorance goes viral.

The Idaho Wolf Problem

In the basement of the capitol
a coal black statue of a screaming
miner stands above a plaque,
dedicated to the 91 men who died
in the obscenely named
Sunshine Mine, 1972, while
their bosses sat in a
shareholder's meeting.

The Academy of Capitalist Ethics:
Entry Examination

On a scale of 1 to 10, how good are you at rationalizing injustice?

The Snow

Before things got difficult for my family,
I complained one Christmas morning
when I didn't get the toy I wanted.
My mother had actually bought it for me,
but she hid it in the closet
to see how I'd react.

Later, when there were no toys,
when there wasn't even a closet,
when my mother had died,
the snow on the ground outside
was enough.

I Read Your Poems in Preston

For Madison

Honey you came out of left
field in a close coat and broke
shoes I watched you watching
your feet walkin down that sad
street in the snow you ate alone
at the chinese place near the
bookstore I read your poems
in Preston and went up past
Mink Creek to the forest with
my old man in our old Dodge
and he fell asleep in the truck
while I watched the wild turkeys
do their best to fly across the river
teach me with your mouth and your
eyes how it is you make a revolution
you cut off your hair you took off your
clothes you wrote a poem of hate for
your father and mother you took a
shower in their shame in the middle
of main street down on your knees burning.
the sun sets via inertia and falls up over the
mountains the same mountains which
gave birth to me in some dark crease I don't
know who you are anymore hiking in the snow
is like making love to a stranger I don't
know who you are anymore and mystery
is the intimacy of god.

Manifest Destiny of the Corporate Dynasty (incorporated)

Judging from my view in front of this concrete
Wal-Mart, I could be anywhere.
Idaho. Utah. Boise. Rexburg. Alberta.

Even the churches here are corporate cookie cutter.
If Brigham Young hadn't been a socialist I'd have
to admit that his prophesy came true:

a theocracy spread through the Rocky Mountains like
wild fire.

Ecosystem of the Wolf

Without a surplus of elk
how will the people
feed their thirst
for blood?

Epilogue to Capitalism

You were wearing red lipstick
and we made love on the brown
carpet in one of the crumbled
palaces of capitalism before we
wandered the aisles of the local
thrift store, the Mexican children picking
through torn stuffed animals, old
women with eye patches buying
beaded necklaces. Eventually we left,
my arms around your shoulders, got into
my dying white car, and drove further
into Idaho.

Big Bill Haywood

for Butch Otter, Mike Crapo, and James Risch

I heard Big Bill is on his way back.
I heard he's gonna beat your ass from
Craters of the Moon all the way to Moscow.
I heard he's gonna drag you overtop of the Sawtooths
by your hair.
I heard he's gonna baptize you in the Bear River.
I heard he's gonna show you what it's like to be poor,
man.
He's gonna show you poverty.

Bear River Massacre

Look out over this valley. Does something seem wrong to you?

Yes.

What is it?

The river has changed places.

Dead Shoshone Winter Encampment

We walk soft between the obscene hot springs in the snow, taste the wet sulfur in the air, follow the blood-red mineral deposits dripping across the barren fields.

The devil has been here, you whisper. *It's so obvious now.*

My Old Man's Cracked Fingertips

Too poor to get unemployment benefits
Too far below the poverty line to receive health care
Too old for that career position
Will work for 8 dollars an hour
Will pay 1,000 dollars as a down payment
Will break my body hauling boxes of fruit
Will do as I'm told
Will apologize for my sins
Will break my body hauling boxes of fruit
Will give my children any money I have
Will break my body hauling boxes of fruit
Will wander my father's old farm
the one he sold to pay the hospital bills
Will find the apple tree he planted near the creek
Will think about my children
Will break my body hauling boxes of fruit
Will sit down in the snow
and kiss my cracked fingertips.

post-post-modern

There is nothing left to do now
but shop
and kill
(when shopping gets boring)

Wolf Carcasses in the Pickup Bed # 1

I thought I saw somethin
pretty in the distance once,
it was a big white mountain.
I wanted to touch it but
the closer I got the
bigger it got and the
prettiness left until
all it was was a bunch of
rocks and trees and so I
never got to touch that mountain,
I never could reach out further
than my hand, and it made me
feel sick in my belly so I
took my rifle and I killed a wolf
I found on that mountain, I let
it bleed out into the snow, I hung
its skin on my wall. I showed it to
all my friends, I showed it to my
wife, I showed it to my boss,
I showed it to my son.

Wolf Carcasses in the Pickup Bed # 2

These bodies aren't your bodies,
or my bodies,
they're just wolf bodies, ya see?
Big dead wolf bodies.
Big son of a bitch, that one, ain't he?
Big alpha male right there.
Damn straight.
It's just a fuckin wolf.
just a big old dead fuckin wolf.
Clipped that one on the hind end,
had to chase her down the side
of the whole fuckin mountain.
yep. I got her though.
I sure did get her.

Winter Camping

Mid-January, Jay and I camped in the place
where the U.S. Government murdered
100 families.

All night I dreamt of my friend Adam Mugleston,
dead for 5 years now, a car wreck on the Teton Pass
on his way home to Idaho.

In the morning, in the warm winter sun,
the land looked as sad and beautiful
as a child.

BYU-Idaho

"Let he that is without sin cast the first stone."

And those sons of bitches all picked up stones.

My Cat is Missing

It's not like Troll Cat – as Madison
and I named him two years ago,
lying beside each other on the
trampoline in the sunshine of the
farm – is anything more than a pet.
Though we did think it was
strange the way he preferred to
live inside a tree, and the way,
after Barbara kicked me
out of the house and he had no
one to care for him for a year,
he still came up to me, kissing
my hands and purring. But life
goes on. Add him to the list of
cats, dogs, snakes, mice,
lizards, salamanders, frogs,
horses, pigs, calves, chickens,
and rabbits I have lost. A list that
grows longer than my hair, longer than
my memory can grasp, a list that bypasses
even my mother, on the bed she would
die on, holding the orphaned kitten
and reminding me: *It misses its mother.*
Do you see how it's sad? Do you miss
your mother? or when Tig, our orange tom,
curled himself up on the spot where
his brother died of distemper, and wept
for three days and three nights, refusing
food and water. The list goes on
and farther than my humanity. Coyote
Moon, sleeping near my feet last night,
woke me up when she left to climb the small
stairwell into the attic. *Where are you going?*
I asked her. There are fields scattered throughout
Eastern Idaho that hold some of the best
people I have known, small white bones,
headstones now lost, graves dug by my
father, slept on now by horses in the sunshine,
the mud fresh and fragrant in their coats.

Fairy Tales

The Catholics told stories
where nature personified evil
to disenfranchise their
pagan subjects.

Well I ain't afraid of the big bad wolf.

Jesus Christ Lives in Idaho

He gained a reputation for talking back to police officers,
for teaching kids to disobey their parents, for telling old
women to lighten up. It got so bad that City Council
had a meeting just to decide what to do about him.
In the end, they got him on trumped up pot charges.
I was there, man, I know it was bull shit.
Since then I hear he took off for the mountains.
I hear he's living near the Snake out there somewhere,
growing out his beard, caring for sick pelicans,
plotting his return.

Anarchism

Come and make love with me,
come and tear off your clothes,
woman, come and throw your body
onto mine, come and embrace the
sounds of our pelvises colliding,
come and erase the dreams I've
been having, come and, for just
a moment, do not feel obliged
to acknowledge my power,
your power, or any power,
and give yourself up, with me,
to THE power.

Five Elk at Franklin Basin

Wild animals remind us the
world exists outside ourselves.
To kill an animal for sport
is to kill the world. To kill
the world is to kill your mother.

Lost man, hell is walking through
a forest and believing that you are
alone.

YELLOW MOUNTAIN COLLECTIVE IS AN INDEPENDENT PRESS OUT OF IDAHO, UTAH, AND ALBERTA.

IT PUBLISHES POETRY, REVOLUTIONARY SOCIAL COMMENTARY, AND SOMETIMES OTHER THINGS TOO.

JOSHUA LEW MCDERMOTT IS A POET FROM RIGBY, IDAHO AND LOGAN, UTAH.

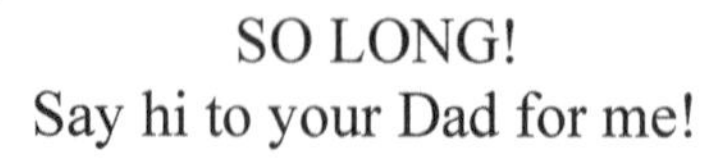
SO LONG!
Say hi to your Dad for me!

www.ingramcontent.com/pod-product-compliance
Ingram Content Group UK Ltd.
Pitfield, Milton Keynes, MK11 3LW, UK
UKHW041901190726
13854UKWH00003B/1014

9 781304 893376